Writing Builders

Rick and Rachel Build a RESEARCH REPORT

by Sue Lowell Gallion
illustrated by Chi Chung

Content Consultant
Jan Lacina, Ph.D.
College of Education
Texas Christian University

NorwoodHouse Press
CHICAGO, ILLINOIS

Norwood House Press
P.O. Box 316598
Chicago, Illinois 60631
For information regarding Norwood House Press, please visit our website at:
www.norwoodhousepress.com or call 866-565-2900.

Editor: Melissa York
Designer: Craig Hinton
Project Management: Red Line Editorial

Library of Congress Cataloging-in-Publication Data
Gallion, Sue Lowell.
Rick and Rachel build a research report / by Sue Lowell Gallion ; illustrated by Chi Chung.
pages cm. -- (Writing builders)
Summary: "Rick has to write his first research report and Rachel helps him. They go to the library and online to find information about the endangered African Black Rhino. Concepts include; revising, scanning and using reliable sources. Activities in the back help the reader organize and write a research report"-- Provided by publisher.
Includes bibliographical references.
ISBN 978-1-59953-583-8 (library edition : alk. paper) -- ISBN 978-1-60357-563-8 (ebook) 1. Report writing--Juvenile literature. I. Chung, Chi, illustrator. II. Title.
LB1047.3.G355 2013
808.02--dc23
2013010267

Manufactured in the United States of America in North Mankato, Minnesota.
233N—072013

Words in **black bold** are defined in the glossary.

Doing Research Step-by-Step

I have a big map on the wall of my room. I draw stars on places I want to visit all over the world. My cousin Rachel wants to go to lots of the same places. We both want to see wild animals in Africa. We'd like to see whales in Alaska too!

But instead of looking at my map, I had a big project to do for school. I had never done a research report before. At first, I was worried that a research report would be hard. But the key to writing a report is working step-by-step. One step at a time, and I know I'll go far . . . maybe even all the way to Africa!

By Rick, age 9

"There's Aunt Lucy!" Rick said. He and his cousin Rachel were waiting outside school for their ride.

"Do you want to go to the park today?" Aunt Lucy asked after Rick and Rachel got into the car.

"I wish I could," Rick said. "But I need to go to the library. My teacher assigned us a research report."

"Well, the key to doing a research report is planning," said Aunt Lucy. "When you first get started, it might seem like a lot of work. But just keep your thoughts and research organized, and you can work step-by-step."

"So what is the first step?" asked Rick.

"You should pick a **topic**," said Rachel.

"We're supposed to learn about an animal," said Rick.

"Maybe you should choose an animal that lives somewhere we want to visit, like Africa!" suggested Rachel.

At the library, Rick and Rachel sat on the floor. They looked at books on animals.

"Elephants? Tigers?" said Rick. "This rhino looks tough."

Rick turned a page. "Rhinos live in more places than just Africa!" he exclaimed. "And there are five different kinds."

"That sounds like a lot to research," said Rachel. "Do you have to do a report on every kind of rhino?"

"Here are the directions from my teacher," Rick said. "First, we choose our topics. Then we're supposed to narrow our focus. I'm not sure what that means."

"That sounds like instead of having many topics, you just pick one." Rachel handed Rick another book.

"My topic is, rhinos are endangered!" exclaimed Rick. "There are less than 5,000 black rhinos living in the wild. I would love to see one! I want to learn why rhinos are endangered. Maybe we can help save them."

"So you've picked your topic?" asked Aunt Lucy, coming back with her own stack of books. "Why don't you make a list of questions you want to answer in your report? Then start gathering information."

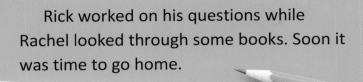

Rick worked on his questions while Rachel looked through some books. Soon it was time to go home.

1. Why are black rhinos endangered?
2. Where could I see a black rhino in the wild?
3. How many black rhinos are left?
4. What can we do to save black rhinos?

"How's your rhino research going?" Aunt Lucy asked the next day. Rick and Rachel were doing homework at Aunt Lucy's kitchen table and having a snack. Rick took a bite of an apple while Rachel sipped her milk.

"We worked in the school library today," replied Rick. "I need to use at least three different sources. The librarian showed us a website to use. I looked in an online encyclopedia and some books too. We need to keep track of our sources to make a bibliography. That's the list at the end of the report that tells where we got our information."

Rick took another bite. "I wrote down my questions on note cards. I found some answers at the library today. I wrote them on my note cards along with the source so I would know where I got the facts too. Now I need to look for more facts. But this book is really long. And it's all about rhinos, not just about saving them."

Rachel took her cup to the sink. “We just learned how to **scan** a book. That means you don’t have to read the whole book to use it for research.”

“How do you do that?” asked Rick. He handed the book to Rachel.

“Look at the table of contents for chapters about why rhinos are endangered or how to save them,” Rachel said. “And you can read the headings on a page to see what it’s about without reading every word. See, here’s a chapter on threats to rhinos. Look at the **index** for similar ideas.”

“Right,” agreed Rick. “Then I can read the important sections more closely.”

“Think of different words that describe what you’re looking for,” added Aunt Lucy. “You might find information under *endangered*, *threats*, or *conservation*, for example.”

TABLE OF CONTENTS
1. Introducing the Rhinoceros
2. Rhinoceros Habitat
3. Rhinoceros Families
4. Threats to the Rhinoceros
5. How to Save the Rhinoceros

“Can you tell us some rhino facts, Rick?” Aunt Lucy asked.

Rick pulled a small stack of note cards out of his backpack and spread them out on the kitchen table. “I learned that black rhinos are often killed for their horns. It seems like such a waste.”

1. Why are black rhinos endangered?

- Poachers are people who kill rhinos and other animals.
- Poachers cut off rhino horns and sell them for lots of money.
- A horn is made of the same stuff as my nails and hair, called keratin.
- Horns are ground up and used for medicine in some countries.
- Black rhinos have two horns. Rhino horns grow back even if you cut them off, but poachers kill rhinos anyway.

2. Where could I see a black rhino in the wild?

- They live in Africa, and their habitat is woodland savanna.
- They live in wildlife reserves for protection.
- Rangers guard rhinos. Wildlife reserves have fences.

3. How many black rhinos are left?

- Less than 5,000 are left in the wild.

4. What can we do to save black rhinos?

- People visiting Africa can help protect black rhinos.
- Money from tourists helps protect rhinos.
- Tourism gives local people jobs so they don't sell rhino horns.
- Organize a school fund-raiser if you can't go to Africa.

Next, Rick pulled a work sheet out of his backpack.

"What's this chart?" asked Rachel.

"My **graphic organizer**. I fill it out next with the main ideas of my report. The questions I asked on my note cards will become my main ideas," answered Rick.

"This will help you decide what facts to use. If a fact doesn't fit, you leave it out of the report," said Aunt Lucy.

"You can switch the order of your original questions now too, if it makes more sense," added Rachel.

"Yes," agreed Rick. "I think I'll cut some facts about rhino horns. That's what rhinos are like, not how we can save them. And I'll switch Question 1 and Question 2. Question 3 only has one point, so I think I'll add it somewhere else."

MAIN IDEA GRAPHIC ORGANIZER
Main idea: There are less than 5,000 black rhinos in the wild.
Details
1. They live in Africa, and their habitat is woodland savanna.
2. They live in wildlife reserves for protection.
3. Rangers guard rhinos. Wildlife reserves have fences.
Main idea: Rhinos are endangered because of poaching.
Details
1. Poachers are people who kill rhinos and other animals.

MAIN IDEA GRAPHIC ORGANIZER

Main Idea: There are less than 5,000 black rhinos in the wild.

Details

1. They live in Africa, and their habitat is woodland savanna.
2. They live in wildlife reserves for protection.
3. Rangers guard rhinos. Wildlife reserves have fences.

Main Idea: Rhinos are endangered because of poaching.

Details

4. Poachers are people who kill rhinos and other animals.
5. Poachers cut off rhino horns and sell them for lots of money.
6. Horns are ground up and used for medicine in some countries.
7. Rhino horns grow back even if you cut them off, but poachers kill the rhinos anyway.

Main Idea: We can help save the black rhino.

Details

8. Money from tourists in Africa helps protect rhinos.
9. Tourism gives local people jobs so they don't sell rhino horns.
10. Organize a school fund-raiser if you can't go to Africa.

MAIN IDEA GRAPHIC ORGANIZER

"Well, I've put all the information I have on the graphic organizer," said Rick.

"Looks like you're ready to write!" congratulated Aunt Lucy.

"I'm kind of worried about that part," Rick admitted.

"Every report has three parts, right?" said Aunt Lucy. "The introduction prepares the reader. The body paragraphs are your arguments—the facts you found in your research. The conclusion reminds readers what you've said."

"Thanks, Aunt Lucy," said Rick. "We have all day tomorrow to work on our reports."

The next day, when Rick and Rachel got in the car, Aunt Lucy asked about Rick's report.

"This morning, we wrote," Rick said. "I put all my facts in order, and I wrote an introduction and a conclusion. This afternoon, we **revised** with a partner. I worked with Sarah. We looked at what I had written again and made changes. I helped Sarah with her report too."

At Aunt Lucy's, Rick pulled out his paper.

"How did you revise your report?" asked Aunt Lucy.

"I changed the order of some sentences. Then I switched out some words to make it sound better. And I found some places to use **linking words**," Rick said.

"I forgot what those are," said Rachel.

"Those are words that connect ideas together," filled in Rick. "Like *also, another, but*, and *because*."

Rick pulled out a page with lots of writing on it. “This is my introduction. I started with a **hook** to catch my readers’ attention. You can see how I revised it too.”

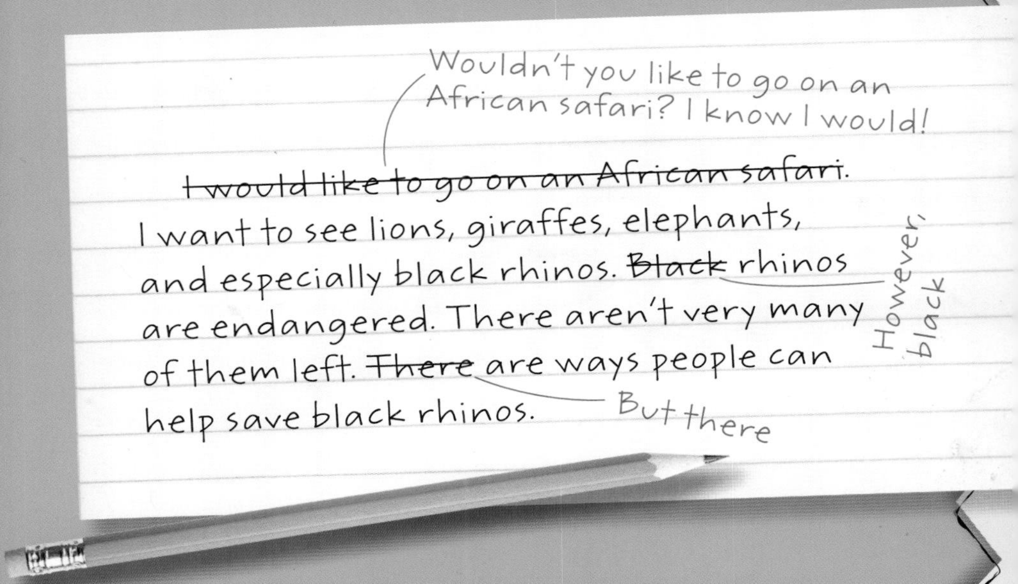
Wouldn’t you like to go on an African safari? I know I would!
~~I would like to go on an African safari~~.
I want to see lions, giraffes, elephants,
and especially black rhinos. ~~Black~~ rhinos
are endangered. There aren’t very many
of them left. ~~There~~ are ways people can
help save black rhinos.
However, black
But there

“That sounds a lot smoother,” said Aunt Lucy. “Linking words keep your writing from being too choppy. Let’s read the rest of your report!”

How to Save the Black Rhino

By Rick

Wouldn't you like to go on an African safari? I know I would! I want to see lions, giraffes, elephants, and especially black rhinos. However, black rhinos are endangered. There aren't very many of them left. But there are ways people can help save black rhinos.

There are less than 5,000 black rhinos in the wild. They live in Africa, and their habitat is the woodland savanna. Woodland savanna is a grassy plain with some trees. Most black rhinos live in wildlife reserves for protection. Wildlife reserves have fences, and rangers who work there guard the rhinos.

The worst enemies of the black rhino are poachers who kill them for their horns. In some countries, people pay a lot of money for rhino horns. They grind them up to make medicine. Rhino horns grow back if they get cut off, but poachers kill rhinos anyway.

We can fight poachers and help save the black rhino. One way is visiting Africa. Money from tourists helps protect black rhinos. Also, tourism gives local people jobs. That way they can make money without selling rhino horns. Even if you can't visit Africa, you can still help the black rhino. One way is to organize a school fund-raiser.

The black rhino is endangered, and it needs our help. Even if you can't go to Africa or raise money, tell everyone you know about the black rhino. If enough people work to help the black rhino, maybe we can save it. And then if I ever get to go on an African safari, maybe I'll see one!

Bibliography

"Rhinoceros Facts." *Monroe City Zoo.* 2013. www.monroecityzoo.com.

"Rhinoceros." *The Big Fun Encyclopedia for Kids.* 2012. www.bfencyclopedia.com.

Sochi, Shelly. *Black Rhino.* New York: Big City Publishers, 2012.

"Wow," said Rachel. "I never knew I could help endangered animals."

"I know," said Rick. "Even kids can make a difference. Let's get started!"

You Can Build a Research Report, Too!

A research report is a great way to share information, whether you're researching potato chips or Pluto.

Step 1. Plan
Choose a topic that interests you. Then think of several questions you want to answer in your report. Note cards will help you stay organized. Try writing each question on a separate note card. Then write down facts that answer the questions.

Write the source, or where you got the information, on the note card. Use only trusted sources. Some Internet sites may not contain correct facts. Keep a list of your sources for your bibliography.

When you're taking notes, write down facts in your own words. Imagine you're telling someone about your topic. Put your note cards in that order. Then use a graphic organizer to build your writing plan.

Step 2. Write
Reports have three parts: introduction, body paragraphs, and conclusion.

Introduction: Start with something snappy! This makes the reader want to know more. Include a topic sentence that tells what your report is about.

Body paragraphs: Each paragraph answers a question about your topic. Here's where you add details.

Conclusion: This reminds the reader of your main idea. Summarize the things you learned. This is a good place to give your opinion.

Your bibliography goes at the end your report. Your teacher will tell you what form to use.

Step 3. Revise
Read your first draft out loud. Does the order make sense? Are you using interesting words? Do your sentences and paragraphs express your ideas clearly? Use linking words (*because, but, since, or, also*) to combine sentences or ideas. Ask a friend to read your report too. He or she might notice something you missed or teach you something new.

Step 4. Publish
Now, rewrite or type your final copy. You may add pictures. Read your final copy to your family so they can learn about your topic too!

Glossary

graphic organizer: a visual form to help you organize your ideas.

hook: a fact, quote, question, or funny story that captures a reader's attention.

index: a list of page numbers where information is found in a book.

linking words: words that connect ideas together, such as *also, another, but,* and *because.*

revised: took a second (or third!) look at your report to make your writing better.

scan: to use the table of contents, headings, or index to find information in a book.

topic: the main area of interest in your report.

For More Information

Books

Asselin, Kristine Carlson. *Smart Research Strategies: Finding the Right Sources*. North Mankato, MN: Capstone Press, 2013.

Fontichiaro, Kristin, and Emily Johnson. *Know What to Ask: Forming Great Research Questions*. Ann Arbor, MI: Cherry Lake Publishing, 2012.

Throp, Claire. *Put It Together: Using Information*. Chicago: Heinemann Library, 2010.

Websites

Kids Click!
http://www.kidsclick.org/
This website has links to trusted sources for many topics.

KidsConnect's Research Toolbox
http://www.ala.org/aasl/aboutaasl/aaslcommunity/quicklinks/k12students/aaslkctools
Research tips from the American Association of School Librarians.

About the Author

Sue Lowell Gallion is a writer who lives in Leawood, Kansas. Just like Rick and Rachel, she loves to travel.